SEASONS

A TALE OF THE UPS AND DOWNS OF GROWING UP

by

Daniel Erdely

DORRANCE
PUBLISHING CO
EST. 1920
PITTSBURGH, PENNSYLVANIA 15238

Dorrance Publishing Co
585 Alpha Drive
Pittsburgh, PA 15238
Visit our website at www.dorrancebookstore.com

ISBN: 979-8-88812-068-2
eISBN: 979-8-88812-568-7

DEDICATION

To my friends from the past who inspired me to be who I became.
To my friends of the present who help me to continue the journey.
And to my beautiful bride who does it all.

ABOUT THE STORY

The story is a fictionalized account of the first season I worked at Waldameer Park in Erie, Pennsylvania. Many of the names have been changed along with the time frame of the story. However, the spirit of the story, the lessons learned there through wonderful, extraordinary people is true. Life, I have found, is as full of ups and downs as a roller coaster. The important thing though is to hold on to the guard rail and keep moving forward.

The Comet is still there and while it is considered small by today's standards, it still manages to thrill. The mega coaster there, the Ravine Flyer 2, has been constructed very close to the route of the first coaster and has an impressive lift hill and an even more impressive drop. I think that might correspond to the bigger challenges of today. The track is still walked and checked and reflective of the age in which we live. The important thing is to hold on to those we love and keep moving forward.

CHAPTER ONE

What a journey this has been. I'm seventy-seven years old now and I spend a lot of time looking back over my life. As with all lives, there are days of profound joy and there are periods of intense sorrow. There are days of regret and days of satisfaction. Everyone's life is like this, but to be content a person must look at the whole, rather than reliving the negatives.

My journey begins with a happy childhood. We lived in the upstairs flat of my grandparent's home on the east side of the Erie, PA. The house was an old Victorian clapboard that had stood on East Tenth Street for over a hundred years. It was the kind of structure that had large public rooms and very small bedrooms. The house had an unusual room configuration that wouldn't make sense today, but we loved the house and my family lived there for over seventy years.

My father worked for a company that made toys. My father, I was proud to say, was one of Santa's helpers. My mother had the responsibility of raising my two brothers and me. We lived a quite ordinary life. My grandparents, who lived downstairs, were always there as part of my life. We kids would run down constantly to see what Busia (grandmother) and Dziadzia (grandfather) were doing or just to sit with them. When my mother's dinner didn't suit my taste, I would run downstairs to see what Busia was cooking. My grandparents living downstairs gave me a comforting sense of security and contentment. I had food, shelter, clothing, and, most importantly, love. I was surrounded by people who cared about me and sheltered me from the stings the outside world could inflict.

In the back of our flat was a large bathroom with a window that looked out to our back yard and beyond the garage at the rear of the yard was an alley that ran the length of the block. I would often look out that window in the late afternoon looking for my father to get home from work. I remember that one time in the evening I was looking out that window, waiting for my parents to return home from a shopping trip. I remember anxiously waiting and waiting, growing more concerned with each passing minute. Finally, I saw the car come down the alley to our garage. To this day, I don't know what caused me to become so upset but the feeling of panic is still there when I think about that night. That back window was like a view of the world beyond my house that was both enticing and frightening at the same time.

I started school and my world started to expand.

I went to a Polish Catholic school and was educated by wonderful nuns. I was a good student and enjoyed school. I was shy and quiet and tried not to bring attention to myself. I was one of the smallest kids in the class and very sheltered living in the bubble of my family. There weren't any kids in my neighborhood, so I learned to enjoy being alone. I got along with my classmates but did not form any long-lasting friendships. I tried my best to be invisible. Most of the other kids in my class were more sophisticated and, to me, somewhat intimidating.

The one day at school that I especially anticipated was the school picnic. Held every year in early June just before the school year ended, it was at Waldameer,, a small amusement park overlooking the lake. My mother and my aunt and cousins would catch the Tenth Street bus that took us to Calvary Cemetery. We would depart the bus walking past the graves, occasionally stopping when my mom or aunt would go past the grave of a relative or friend. We would head for the gate and there across the road was the entrance to what I considered the most wonderful place in the whole world.

I fell in love with Waldameer. My mom and dad would take my brothers and me to the park and we would go on the merry-go-round or the train ride.

We'd also like to look at the monkeys on Monkey Island in the park. The island was surrounded by a moat. We would throw popcorn or peanuts and see the monkeys ingeniously fish the goodies out of the water. The sound of the carousel music reverberated in my ears as I stood there feeding the monkeys. To this day, occasionally the melodies of those songs still resonate in my mind. It was, to me, a magical place that I never wanted to leave.

Looking out the bathroom window, in the distance, was a house a couple of blocks away that reminded me of the merry-go-round. I convinced myself that I was seeing Waldameer Park. It was fun imagining that all I had to do to see this wonderful place was look out the bathroom window and there it was, the most magical place in the world.

Waldameer Park was situated on a bluff overlooking Lake Erie. At one time there had been access to the beach down below. There was a huge bathhouse, snack bar, and canoes to rent for boating on the lagoon. These had all been destroyed many years ago by a great storm that washed away the beach and all the facilities.

The park survived because it also had a ballroom, The Gardens. Here famous big bands would serenade dancers with the biggest hits of the day. If the weather was cooperative, guests during intermission could leave the ballroom and go into the amusement park for snacks or maybe even a ride on the carousel or if the couple was daring enough on the Ravine Flyer. The Flyer was a huge wooden coaster that followed the terrain and literally flew up and down through the wooded ravine. It was recognized as one of the best coasters anywhere in the country.

All that was in the past, however, because the big band era ended and times and tastes change. The Ravine Flyer was torn down after a fatal accident. A young man had fallen from the ride after it had stalled and stopped at the bottom of an incline. The terrain was very hilly, and he fell down to the bottom of the ravine and died. Mrs. Mueller, the owner of the park, ordered the ride to be removed as a result.

The park as I knew it had only eight major rides, several kiddie rides, a refreshment stand, an arcade, and a string of carnival like games. There was also a fortune teller who looked mysterious and foreboding in front of her stand. The park also had a miniature golf course. This was the park as I knew and loved. There were bigger parks not too far away, but none had a place in my heart like Waldameer Park.

School picnics kept the park busy through the early part of June. My picnic was always held during the first week of June. My cousins and I would spend the day running from ride to ride, anxious to experience every one of the rides. We would enjoy a candy apple or a cotton candy in between. The one ride I did not go on was the Comet. This was a small roller coaster that filled the need for the park to have a coaster. It may have been small, but picking up on my mother's apprehension, it seemed too terrifying for me.

My mother told the story of her experience on the Ravine Flyer. She had been on a date with some young suitor who suggested they ride the behemoth coaster. Reluctantly, she agreed. As the coaster train sped down the first hill, my mom in her fright had grabbed hold of the young man and had managed to pull off every button on his shirt. That potential romance fizzled. Also, my mother vowed never to ride a roller coaster again. The Ravine Flyer is no more, having been replaced by the smaller, more sedate Comet roller coaster.

My cousins would tease me and challenge me to ride The Comet, but I always managed to avoid going on it. My mother's story from the Ravine Flyer haunted me and kept me away from riding it.

The eight years at St. Stans will forever be etched in my being as extremely happy and fulfilling. School picnics at Waldameer Park were a big part of those happy memories. The wonderful nuns who educated me made sure I was prepared for my next adventure.

I was fortunate to be accepted as a student at Cathedral Preparatory School for Boys. High school is undoubtedly a challenging time for everyone. My memories of high school are not very good. I had a poor self-image that contributed to a natural shyness. In my quest to be invisible at Prep, I was often challenged. When roll was called in a class, I would position myself as far back in the room as possible and whisper in a tremulous voice, "Present." I despised the sound of my voice. Recent to this time, I had heard a tape of my speech. I was horrified. It sounded awful so I decided to speak as little as possible.

The swim class was another serious problem. At Prep, we swam in the nude. Nude swimming was very common for boys. It was not unusual in many schools. In ninth grade, boys can be very different. Some are more developed than others. I recall my first time standing there with a group of thirty boys stark naked. Some of the guys were smooth and bare while others were hairy everywhere. The kid next to me was tall and very hairy.

He poked me and with a sneer on his face and said, "Look at those two smoothies there. I'll bet they can't even get it up yet."

Boys can be cruel to one another often with unmerciful razzing. I was fortunate to have at least sufficient hair down below saving me from a lot of torment. I was also afraid of going in the water. To this day, I do not know how to swim and avoid swimming pools.

In the locker room, I would dress as quickly as possible in order to escape any possible comments about my appearance. I was always careful never to make eye contact with anyone. This was another indication of the challenges high school would present.

The problem with swimming nude though was that I was skinny, really skinny. I had bones protruding on my shoulders. My legs were scrawny. My chest looked like I could have escaped from a prisoner of war camp. I could have been an advertisement for what would happen if you didn't take your vitamins and eat properly. I was about five-feet eight-inches tall and barely weighed a hundred pounds. The problem was that I just didn't like to eat. My mother was a good cook, but I would just nibble at my food.

I dreaded looking in a mirror or having my picture taken. Every bodily flaw in my mind was enhanced. I was sure people laughed when they saw me. All in all, I felt being invisible, sitting as far away from the teacher as possible, and not talking to others was the best way to survive high school.

I was extremely skinny, had a horrible sounding voice, looked ridiculous, had a limited IQ, and was not an interesting person. The only positive I could think of as I began high school was that I had hairy balls.

The mantra of Prep was to develop the student in mind, body, and soul. The school had a reputation of excelling in all three areas, but particularly in sports. The school fielded teams in football, basketball, baseball, wrestling, and track and field sports, as well as golf and tennis. I never played or even considered participating in any of them. My family was not interested in sports and as a result, I was never exposed to them. My elementary school did have a basketball team that played in a Catholic league, but it never entered my mind to participate in it.

Mr. Ski was the ninth-grade gym instructor. He was a big, mean looking hulk of a man with a long Polish name that even with my Polish language background I found intimidating. This was my initial introduction to physical education. I had the feeling Mr. Ski and I were not compatible.

We lined up in three rows of ten. Naturally, I positioned myself in the back row behind a big chunky kid. Our first exercise was to be jumping jacks. *What the heck are jumping jacks?* I thought to myself. I watched the guys around me and began to jump and spread my legs. Somehow though, I realized I could not coordinate my leg movement with my arms. I decided for visibility purposes it was best to move the hands and not move my legs. It seemed to work. Mr. Ski had not noticed this uncoordinated bumpkin in the back row.

Our next activity was push-ups. We were to do twenty-five. I placed myself in position and attempted to do one as instructed. I couldn't. *How can I fake this?* I wondered. I got on my knees and tried pushing up. It worked. I never did do the twenty-five expected, but I had managed to do three. Success, I managed not to get Mr. Ski's attention. He was focused on some kid up front who had been fooling around. Could I get away with this all year?

The rest of the class was a blur. At the end of the period, he divided us into two groups for a basketball game. It was to be shirts versus the skins. *Please God let me be shirts.* My prayer answered, a team captain was chosen to pick the initial players. He looked at me and I could immediately see that he'd never pick me. Hooray! Mr. Invisibility survives.

The rest of the morning went by quickly. There was algebra taught by a sweet looking young nun followed by civics class taught by Mr. McGovern, the football coach. I noticed he didn't seem focused on civics but on the sports page in the newspaper that sat on the desk in front of him. My fourth period was Latin. Father Rush was a kindly, intellectual looking priest who loved Latin and tried in this the first class to get us motivated and interested. Veni, vidi, vici. I still recall reading Julius Caesar's account of his time in Gaul. We also had theology taught by a young, newly ordained priest. I was pleased that I arrived at each class on time being able to navigate my way around the huge building.

Lunch time at last. All the freshmen ate lunch together in the basement cafeteria. As usual, I went to the furthest part of the room behind the Coke vending machine, taking my place at the empty table and hoping no one else would join me there.

A skinny, dark haired, tall kid wandered over.

"Anybody sitting here?" he inquired.

Michael entered my life.

CHAPTER TWO

My attempt at invisibility had been thwarted by Michael, who without hesitation sat down and introduced himself. Within a few minutes, I learned he lived a few miles away from me, that he had two brothers, one older and one younger, and that he was from Holy Family parish. In the Erie, you were identified by your parish. The city was divided into ethnic sections. There was a Polish area, a German area, an Italian section, and so on. Mike was from a Slavic area.

Lunch time went by rapidly and Mike suggested we exchange phone numbers. I was surprised but agreeable. He said on our way back to our respective classes that he enjoyed lunch with me and would see me tomorrow.

The next day, he came to my table again and I felt free to chatter about anything and everything. I was comfortable enough to remove my invisibility cloak and relax. I discovered two important things about Mike that day. First that he loved Shelley Fabares on the *Donna Reed Show* and secondly that he loved Waldameer Park. Now I felt even better about Mike. It was like I found a compatriot who shared my likes and dislikes. He was someone I didn't need to be intimidated by or uncomfortable being with at school.

We started to call each other each evening especially right after the *Donna Reed Show*. "Wow, did you see Shelley tonight! Wasn't she hot?" was a typical conversation starter. We also talked about school discussing teachers and events at Prep. Boys probably gossip as much or more than girls.

Gym and swim class were still my big challenges at Prep. One day I heard that if you were in the marching band, you were excused from physical education. The theory being that the marching would count as the state required exercise regime. I never played any instrument and my knowledge and interest in music were miniscule, but this sounded like an opportunity to be free of Mr. Ski and Phys Ed.

Mr. Cavelli was the director of music. He was a handsome older gentleman who was always dressed impeccably, exuding a great degree of elegance and charm. He was well-known throughout the area because he and his brother led a band that played every church dance, wedding, or other events like that in the city. His band had that "big band" sound of Glenn Miller or the others of that era. He also led the band that performed every Sunday evening at the pavilion at the city's largest park.

The Prep marching band was, as with everything else at Prep, expected to be the best in the city. The band had the snazziest uniforms and the most well-known music director. It was also one of the largest bands in the city. Prep had about fifteen hundred students and was considered the most prestigious school in the area.

I got permission to go see Mr. Cavelli during one study hall period. I was hoping to get a position, any position, with the marching band. Perhaps they needed somehow to help care for the uniforms or someone to help with the band instruments. I was willing to help in any way possible to get out of gym.

Maybe I could be in the color guard. These were the students who carried the flags and marched in front of the band. There were also two students on either side of the flag bearers who carried realistic rifles. My lack of musical knowledge would certainly not be an impediment to being in the color guard. I could do that easily!

I was accepted as a color guard member and as a result my schedule would be changed, eliminating the physical education classes. I was ecstatic! I was free of Mr. Ski. No more jumping jacks. My aversion to swimming was protected and my modesty was protected! I would, I thought, become the best color guard member that ever marched with the Prep band.

A few weeks later, Mr. Cavelli asked me if I ever played or was interested in playing a musical instrument. He told me that the band was weak in trombone players and he was looking for students who would be interested in learning to play it. I jumped at the opportunity. This would ensure that I would be free of gym class for my entire Prep years.

I never became a very good trombone player. In a concert performance, I could manage to perform well enough so as not to draw attention to my lack of musical ability. What I never did master was marching and playing at the same time. My lack of coordination was overwhelming. I could either march in step or play the instrument while fumbling along. I chose early on to march while faking the playing. One does learn to survive!

Mike and I had become best buddies. In fact, he was my only friend. My fear of interaction with the other students continued throughout my entire four years at Prep. During the summer, Mike and I often went to Waldameer Park. We didn't drive then, so we took the bus. We never had a lot of money to spend but we would be content to get a Coke and play some of the machines in the arcade. I was grateful that I had a good friend who shared my interests. Having a best buddy like Mike was a valuable gift.

We also went to the beach frequently. We would walk from my house to State Street and down State to the public dock. There we would take the ferry (for twenty-five cents) across the bay to the peninsula. We spread out our blanket, got out our portable radio, took out the deck of cards we brought, and spent the rest of the afternoon playing Hearts or War or any other card game we could imagine. Oh yes, we also watched girls!

Neither one of us were skilled at impressing girls. Mike was much better at it then I was in that he liked to talk to everyone. I was far more reserved. Sometimes, if some girl spoke to me, I would stammer a bit while turning a bright crimson. I do not recommend this as an approach to meeting girls.

We were now in our junior year of high school. Everyone was getting their driver's permit, including Mike. My parents never mentioned it. I waited and they never approached me about getting my driver's permits I could not understand why they did not seem eager for me to get mine. Finally, I approached them about it. I was told that they could not at this time put me on their insurance policy because my older brother was on their car insurance policy.

They could not afford to have another driver at this time. I was shattered. It was a real blow to my ego to see everyone else in my class driving but me.

The fact that I did not have my driver's license caused me to feel more diminished. Mike was now driving so we always had transportation, but I wished that I would have been able to alternate driving instead of always having to rely on him for a ride.

One day soon after, Mike arrived at my house unexpectantly driving a dark green 1956 Thunderbird. Mike's dad had gotten him an early (one year early) graduation gift. Despite being excited for Mike, this didn't make me feel better about myself. Mike's having a car made our adventures together more exciting and expansive. We were now able to really spread our wings!

I was beginning to feel more repressed at Prep. I didn't especially like my teachers and as a result, my grades reflected my attitude. I passed everything with barely passing grades. I felt defeated and lacked any impetus to improve.

One day at the end of the day, I went to my locker as usual to get my coat and whatever books I might need to study from for the next day. As I approached my locker, a guy I'd never seen before stood blocking my locker while he had the adjacent locker open. I had never seen anyone at that locker before and was surprised to see someone there. I said hello and asked if he could kindly move so I could get into my locker. He gave me a scowl and continued to block my use of it.

"I'll only be a minute," I pleaded.

He gave me a push and told me to go to hell. Other guys nearby started to laugh and taunt me. I went to the bathroom and waited for ten minutes or so before returning to my locker. He was gone along with my ego.

The next day I moved all my books and school paraphernalia to Mike's locker. I'd rather switch than fight. To this day, I can't recall ever seeing this guy before or after this incident. I stayed using Mike's locker for a couple of months before going back to my own. Mike now became my bodyguard. I never had another incident like this, but I knew that everyone regarded me as an oddball. I didn't socialize with anyone but Mike. I didn't belong to any club or group. I left school each day as quickly as I could escape.

Summer came and I could relax. Mike and I continued our forays to Waldameer Park as well as our beach days. I think we both realized that this could be our last "free" summer. We were free of responsibilities and able to do as we pleased. We went to the movies frequently as well as bowling. When I ran out of funds, Mike would pay my way without hesitation.

Mike had met a girl named Jill. He started to spend a lot of time with her. I admit that I did resent Jill taking up so much of his time, especially on weekends. Saturday nights we usually went to the movies. In the Gem City there were only three first run theaters. If a movie was held over, it meant we were left without a choice. Mike and I for example saw *Operation Petticoat* three Saturdays in a row! This was all before Jill who now preoccupied his time and attention.

Jill had arranged a date for me. We were to spend a Saturday afternoon at the beach and then eat at the diner. Mike had talked her into this so I could be included and not be alone on a Saturday. I wasn't sure how I felt about the arrangement. I had dated on other occasions but had never really been serious about any of the girls. In fact, a couple of the young ladies got to me through my mother. The girl's equivalent to Prep was St. Mary's Academy. My mother was friends with their mothers and so I was hooked into going with these young ladies to dances at St. Mary's.

On Saturday, Mike's T-Bird pulled up in front of my house with Jill pressed against Mike as if I would try to steal him away. I squeezed in the back seat. The rear seat was very tight. The car was not made for four people. We headed to pick up my date, Chrissy.

Chrissy was a public. That meant that she did not attend one of the Catholic high schools. Jill had known her from their years together at St. Barbara's Elementary School. She described her as a "live wire who was a little wild." *Oh my*, I thought.

Chrissy was a buxom brunette. She was attractive and every inch "a live wire". She certainly wasn't shy and acted as if I had known her forever. She snuggled next to me and grabbing my hand she pressed it against her leg as we headed to the beach. *Oh my*, I thought.

Bikinis were the newest rage. Wearing one was a sign of a new freedom. "She wore a teeny, weeny yellow polka dot bikini" meant a new age was starting. Jill and Chrissy bore wore bikinis. They weren't teeny weeny like you would find on any beach today and yet it was considered quite daring for that day The girls felt quite courageous and modern and I must admit to being an enthusiastic admirer. *Oh my,* I thought.

We spread out our beach blanket, positioned our radio, and got out the cards while listening to Shelley Fabares singing her hit song, "Johnny Angel".

Chrissy rolled on her stomach, "Would you put some lotion on my back, please?" she asked.

I complied.

"Don't forget the back of my legs too," she whispered.

"Okay," I said. *Oh my,* I thought.

We played cards that hot afternoon. I was sweating partly from the sun, but mostly because of Chrissy. She was an aggressive card player and very smart. She laughed a lot and enjoyed roundly beating us!

Mike and Jill were cuddled together very distracted from the game. The time came to pick up our blanket and pack up for dinner. The girls took their backpacks and headed for the changing room. *Oh my,* I thought. Mike and I merely had to slip on our shorts over our trunks, put on a shirt, and we were ready.

The Glenwood Diner was as usual, very busy. We had to wait about twenty minutes before being seated. Jill and Chrissy were busy chattering while Mike and I stood silently waiting for our table. Chrissy suddenly grabbed my hand and pressed it against her chest.

"I'm having a real good time," she whispered.

Oh my, I thought.

After eating the usual teenage diet of burgers, fries and Cokes, we headed back to the car to go home. Mike suggested taking Chrissy home first as she was the furthest distance from our homes. I walked her to her front door when she suddenly grabbed me and kissed me. It was not just a gentle, sweet kiss, but rather a passionate, aggressive smooch. My ego was inflated as we said goodbye and I headed back to the car. In my mind I heard Shelley Fabares singing "Danny Angel!" Oh my!

I talked to Chrissy a few times afterwards on the phone. However, we never saw each again. I really don't know why except that life sometimes complicates things and time marches on.

CHAPTER THREE

The end of that summer was the end of my age of innocence. Autumn meant my senior year at Prep. It was the dividing line between a carefree existence and a new sense of responsibility and challenges. There were life choices to be made. Everyone in my family was expected to attend college. My Uncle Al, the youngest son of Polish immigrant parents, was the first to seek higher education. He set the stage for all the grandchildren to imitate him and continue their educations.

Gannon College was founded by the bishop of the Gem City as a means of providing educational opportunities to all in our community. My older brother was finishing up his college years. He had been in the Marine Corps and immediately upon his return to civilian life, he started college. I was expected to follow and enroll at Gannon. My grades were less than I was capable of earning, but I had basically given up at Prep and was hoping merely to get through my senior year without failing at any subject. I sent in my application letter and then began the anxious wait for the response.

When I looked over my schedule for the year, I noticed that I was assigned to an advance math class that included calculus. My interest and ability in math was limited. I barely passed geometry and my work in algebra was certainly barely adequate. I went to the office to plead to be reassigned to another math program.

"Unfortunately," the class advisor said, "There are no other classes available. We're confident you can manage it."

My stomach churned in reaction. Didn't they see my record? Math was always my weakest subject. How would this affect my college application if I failed the course?

I also worried about having to decide on a college major. I wasn't mechanically inclined, nor was I good in math. That eliminated engineering. I had no artistic or musical talent. Internally, my mind was constantly considering the possibilities. It suddenly struck me that my carefree days of the past few summers had ended. My life was about to change forever.

Mike and Jill were still very much a couple, even though Jill's mother continuously attempted to thwart the relationship. She just didn't like Mike no matter how hard he tried to please her by presenting himself as a very polite, charming young man.

My experience with meeting girls still had not improved. It seemed like the girls I attracted never connected with my expectations. Sally was sweet, but homely. Allison was pretty, but dumb. Melissa just wanted to get someone to marry. Perhaps my expectations were too high and as a result, while Mike and Jill were out on Saturday nights, I was home alone listening to Shelly Fabares singing "Johnny Angel".

Summer went by quickly. The new school year, my last at Prep, was about to begin. Except for calculus, my schedule did not seem overwhelming. I was determined to finally apply myself to my studies instead of just drifting along. A new year with a new attitude, I promised myself.

One thing that didn't change was my desire to be invisible. I always went to the back of the room as far away from the instructor as possible. I would never raise my hand or even look the teacher in the eyes. When I felt the instructor looking at me or in my direction, I would look down at my desk. I realized soon into the new term that after three years at Prep I really didn't know anyone except Mike. It was like I was a stranger visiting the school for the first time.

I was a poor kid surrounded by guys who had better clothes, who played golf and tennis at the country club, who traveled all over the world and who drove shiny, expensive cars. Here I was without a driver's license and dependent on my best friend, Mike, to go places. I couldn't wait to graduate and move on in life.

I had given up asking about getting a license. Every time I had asked about it was the same response. "Not yet," my dad would say. I realized that there would be no driver's license before graduation. I was sure that everyone else in class had their licenses and some, like Mike, even had their own car. If I remained invisible, no one would know.

Every November, the senior class sponsored a harvest dance. It was always held at the Gardens at Waldameer Park. There was always an orchestra usually it was Mr. Cavelli's band that was well known in the city for sounding very much like those big bands of an earlier age. The ballroom would be decorated with a fall theme and except for the prom in May, this was considered the social event of the year.

Mike, of course, had already asked Jill. My prospect of finding a date was dim. I had crossed the girls I had dated off my list and they reciprocated in a like manner while probably warning other girls to stay away. Mike tried to help as did my mother. My mom suggested I asked Mary Kay, the daughter of my parent's good friends.

Mary Kay was beautiful. She attended the exclusive girl's Catholic Prep school in the swanky west side of the city. There was no way I would ask her. I felt she was out of my league entirely. Needless to say, I did not have the courage to even try.

With no date, the only thing left for me to do was to volunteer to work the dance. The night of the Harvest Ball, a few of the boys without dates had volunteered to collect admission tickets and serve pizza and beverages. I joined that small group of eight guys, who I was not surprised did not have dates either. Working with this group did not help my self-image. I had never even seen any of them previously and it dawned on me that there were other invisible students in my class. I was not alone!

My task was to slice the pizzas and put each piece on a plate along with a couple of autumn decorated napkins. While working at my assignment, I did not at first notice the man standing behind me in the kitchen. One of the guys I was working with told me later that the man was Mr. Nielson, the owner of Waldameer Park. He had looked around the kitchen making sure everything was in order. I wanted to tell him how much I loved his park but before I could, he left and disappeared in the crowd.

After an hour or so, the pizza rush was over. I soon was able to look around and enjoy the sights and sounds around me. The orchestra's sound was overwhelming. It was as if nothing else existed and the music was just for you. The lights in ballroom were dim. The atmosphere romantic. I wished there would have a girl with me to partake of this sublime moment.

I saw Mike and Jill dancing and they looked like a couple deeply in love. They left the dance floor and rushed over to say, "Hi." Jill was beautiful in a dress that reflected the autumn decor. Mike looked handsome in a navy-blue suit. We laughed and chatted a few minutes before they returned to the dance floor.

There was no question that I felt jealous. Everyone was having fun and enjoying the wonderful atmosphere while I was dateless and serving pizza. I felt like a loser. To top it off, when the dance was over, I had to call my dad to come and pick me up. I was a loser.

CHAPTER FOUR

Dr. Tower was my calculus instructor. He was a very handsome, grey-haired priest who looked like he could be a film star. He spoke very softly in a monotone voice. Sitting in the back of the room, sometimes it was almost impossible to hear what he was saying. He would be seated at his desk the entire period, never getting up to use the chalkboard. Occasionally, he would smile and chuckle about something he had just said, but I never understood or heard the comment. He never called on anyone in the class, but just droned on with his lecture. I realized I was in trouble.

I had absolutely no idea what he was talking about. It was as if he were speaking a foreign language. Try as hard as I could, I felt completely lost and overwhelmed. My first problem was concerning the purpose of calculus. I had no idea what calculus meant to do. It didn't look good for my prospects of passing the course. Dr. Tower never assigned homework but would tell us what to read and study from the text.

The textbook entitled *An Introduction to Calculus* was filled with charts, facts, and figures that made absolutely no sense to me. I was the person who barely passed geometry and calculus seemed impossible. Dr. Tower never mentioned an exam. The semester was going by and I got more bewildered by the course with each passing day and I wondered how I was going to be evaluated. I absolutely needed to pass. My college entrance depended on it.

At mid-semester, I was confident all my evaluations in the other subjects would be much improved over previous years. It was even possible, I thought, that I might be able to earn second honors. That meant that all my grades were B level or above. My only worry was my grade in calculus.

Mike and I would still get together as often as possible. Jill's mother would concoct all sorts of activities to prevent her from seeing Mike on most weekends. It seemed to be working. The spark between Mike and Jill seemed diminished.

I returned home one afternoon in early December to see my mother holding a letter addressed to me from Gannon College.

"Open it!" she said anxiously.

I stood holding it for what seemed like forever. My hands were shaking as I tore open the envelope. Silently, I stood there reading the letter.

"What does it say?" my mother yelled.

I broke out in a smile that conveyed the answer. "I'm in!"

There was never a question or doubt that Mike would be accepted to Gannon His grades were consistently high even though he never really worked very hard on his classes. It didn't hurt also that Mike charmed all his instructors with a smiling personality.

In April, I realized the senior prom was almost here and again I had no real girlfriend. I would go to the Saturday night mixers and my cousin, Jacki, would always introduce me to some girl. We would dance and chat, but I was getting nowhere with my dating life. I was starting to despair of finding a date.

Once again, my mother suggested I call Mary Kay. She promised to do a little promoting for me to Mary Kay's mother. Discouraged, but desperate, I agreed.

"Hi," I said as Mary Kay answered the phone. "I was wondering," I whispered in an almost quivering voice, "if you would like to go to the Prep prom with me?"

A long pause followed.

Finally, she responded, "I guess so."

It wasn't an enthusiastic affirmation, but rather an answer of compliance. My mother and her mother had arranged this date.

The prom was always in early May. I was excited and looked forward to it, but a little apprehensive about going with Mary Kay. I decided to rent a powder blue formal jacket rather than the usual white dinner jackets that I expected everyone else to wear that evening. It was the first time I'd ever wear formal wear and I wanted to look my best. I used plenty of Brylcreem to keep my wild hair in place and even though there wasn't a lot to shave, I went over my sparse beard twice before spraying my cheeks with plenty of Old Spice. I was determined to look good and smell good.

Mike was going to pick me up before getting Jill. He had washed the old T Bird and it was glistening. We were on our way to what I hoped would be a great, memorable evening.

We picked up Jill who looked stunning in her pink gown and wearing a white flower in her red hair. Now, we were on our way to pick up Mary Kay. I rang the bell and her mother answered the door. She told me Mary Kay would be down in a few minutes. When she finally appeared, she was wearing an off-white gown along with an unfriendly scowl on her face.

"Let's go," she said almost sounding like, "Let's get this over with as quickly as we can". We drove to the ballroom with Mike and Jill chattering away. Mary Kay hardly looked at me and barely said anything.

The theme of this year's prom was "south seas adventure". The ballroom was decorated with Palm trees and tropical flowers. It was beautiful. Mr. Cavelli's orchestra was on stage and had already started playing and the romantic sound of love songs filled the air.

We picked an unoccupied table not far from the stage. It was a table for six which meant there was room for another couple to join us. Jill and Mike were already off to the dance floor. I asked Mary Kay if she wanted to dance. She smiled and said she'd be right back. She needed to visit the restroom. There I sat alone and waiting. It seemed like she was gone for an eternity. When she returned, she suggested that we get some sodas because she was parched. The line for the refreshments was long and when I returned to the table. there was no one there. I set the Cokes on the table and wondered where Mary Kay had gone.

"She's in the bathroom," Mike said when they came back to the table. I wondered to myself if she was not feeling well because I'd never met anyone who spent so much time in the bathroom.

The rest of the evening continued in the same way. After Jill went to the restroom, I asked her if she'd seen Mary Kay there.

"Oh yes," she replied, "She was smoking up a storm in there. I'm surprised they allow smoking in the bathrooms."

We eventually did get to do one dance together and it was like I was dancing with a cold fish.

After the dance, we went to the Glenwood Diner for breakfast. Mary Kay did have a hearty appetite and ordered a full breakfast which she unapologetically devoured. We drove her home and I walked her to her front door. Barely saying, "Good night," she opened the door and went inside. My "Some Enchanted Evening" ended as *The Night of the Living Dead.* I went home, took off my tux, went into the bathroom and looked out the back window. It looked black and I could barely see my imaginary "merry-go-round" house. Was this what I could expect from seeing and experiencing the world?

The school year was almost over and still we had not had any exam in my calculus course. I had no idea how Dr. Tower was going to grades. Finally, near the last week of school he announced there would be an exam the following day. Now I was in a complete panic. That night I reread almost every page of the text. I still had very little idea of what calculus was and how to use its methodology. I spent the rest of that night praying that somehow, I might get through this course.

The day of the final was a day of anxiety and angst. Dr. Tower passed out the test. It consisted of one problem. We had forty-five minutes to solve it and present our method of achieving the answer. I felt doomed. I don't remember my answer to this challenge, nor do I recall how I got the answer I came up with. I only know that I scribbled some numbers and did some mathematical operation that made it look like I had absorbed something from the class despite Dr. Tower's monotone, boring teaching style.

Graduation day was near. I knew I had passed all my other subjects and in fact, was hoping for second honors. Only Calculus stood in the way. If I failed this class, I would need to go to summer school before I would earn a diploma. My future was in balance.

Our grades were mailed to our homes so each day I would rush home to see if the report card had arrived. On the Thursday right before graduation day, I saw that D-Day had arrived. With sweaty, shaking hands I tore open the letter and quickly looked for the Calculus grade. My mom waited anxiously for my response. There it was in front of me. My grade for calculus was a D. I was in reality relieved. I had passed without knowing how I had done it. It may not have been pretty, but at least I had passed and would graduate on Saturday.

There was no question that I was disappointed by my grades. Before I was assigned to the calculus class, I had even envisioned second honors. My biggest disappointment was my grade in French. My instructor, Professor Cobert, had seemed to like me and my grades were pretty good. My final was just below the level necessary for second honors. I kept thinking, "merde, merde", which is French for... I'll leave it to your imagination, or you can ask Mr. Google.

Mike shared his grades when we spoke that afternoon. He had made first honors and was ranked number seven in the class I had yet not even looked at my class rank. I wasn't sure I wanted to know.

The big day had finally arrived. The weather was a beautiful late spring day with not a cloud in the sky. This meant that the ceremony could be held on the great lawn in front of the school. I got in my rented tux and was ready to go.

Most people remember in detail significant days like graduation day. I do not recall anything that happened next. I do not remember when student two hundred and twelve marched up to get his diploma from the bishop. It was over. I had survived.

I do remember walking to my parents' car and turning around for one last look at the gray stone edifice that had educated me in more ways than one. I believe I was now no longer the naive innocent I had been in my freshman year. I was now more seasoned to begin the next phase of my life.

CHAPTER FIVE

Mike called the following Monday and suggested we take the ferry over to the state park and spend the day at the beach. The old T-Bird was in the garage for a few days, needing new brakes and tires. He thought this would be fun.

"Just like the old days," he said.

I packed up my backpack with my beach necessities, lotion, portable radio, playing cards, blanket and my latest copy of *The Saturday Review*. I put on my trunks under my shorts, told my mom my plans, and went outside to wait for Mike. His aunt, as in the old days, pre-T-Bird, had driven him to my house. We decided to walk the few blocks to the public dock to get the ferry.

The ferry ran each weekday from the dock to the state park. It was cheap, eighty cents one way, and reliable. The ride on the bay was soothing with the cooling breeze and shiny sun. It was an idyllic way to spend a summer day. We spread out the blankets, turned up the radio, splashed on some lotion, and were ready to spend a quiet, relaxing afternoon.

I told Mike that there might not be many days like this left. I started to look for a job. Mike was shocked. It seems he never considered that as a possibility.

"Good luck," he said in a disappointed voice.

Mike's parents had been bankrolling him all these years and had never suggested that he find a job. My parents were not that financially secure. My dad would often be furloughed during the early summer when the toy plant switched over to the production of its Christmas toys. He would always find some temporary employment, but financially this would be a challenging time for our family.

I depended for my money on my grandfather and my Uncle Al. My grandfather was always willing to contribute a fiver to my pocket. My Uncle Al lived in Cleveland and would almost always come home on the weekend. He was the college grad of the family and was working as an accountant at a big company in the big city. He would generously contribute to my entertainment budget. I realized though that I now needed to start earning my own money rather than being entirely dependent on others. I needed a job.

The Erie was not a great place to be looking for employment. The industrial base of the city was dying with many of the old factories standing idle and abandoned. The want ads of the local paper did not provide much encouragement. Men were needed to cut grass or as truck drivers. There was a need for newspaper carriers and musicians for a band. Maybe I could apply, even though I was barely able to play the trombone. I could play the "Colonel Bogey March" if I was sitting. I judged there wouldn't be much demand for my trombone playing.

The ad was near the bottom of the help wanted classifieds. It said that help was wanted at Waldameer Park, all positions available. This would be a dream come true, considering how I loved the place. The only problem was that it was far away and not driving, nor having a vehicle, it would be a challenge getting back and forth to home. I continued to search the classifieds, hoping to find something that I could easily get to and from without depending on my parents for transportation.

An ad for a company called Manpower caught my eye. This was a short-term job placement agency. If a business needed a clerk for a few days, this company would provide it. I thought it would be perhaps something that I could do with the stipulation that the assignment would be within a reasonable walking distance or at least convenient to transportation. I went to their office, filled out the application form, and went home, hoping for a call.

The next morning, my mother woke me saying there was a phone call for me. It was the secretary from Manpower telling me to come to the office to get my first assignment. It was for a landscaping position. I got dressed quickly and almost ran to the office, excited over the prospect that I was soon going to become a verified wage earner. I was given the address and told that it was a job that should take only four hours. The address was a wealthy part of town in a section of old huge mansions. Mrs. Rush needed a "boy" to assist with her gardening. I had been hoping for a full day's work, but at least it was a start. The pay was five dollars an hour which made me excited to earning my first twenty dollars!

Mrs. Rush lived a magnificent brick house that dominated the area around it. It had a huge wrap around porch with large potted ferns resting on the porch's wall. Some of the windows were stain glass and the front door was a magnificently carved work of art. I rang the bell with a little apprehension, not knowing what to expect nor knowing precisely what my job would be.

The lady who answered was a short, well-dressed older woman probably in her late seventies. She told me to go around to the rear of the house and she would show me my assignment. The back yard was quite large for a city lot and had a spectacular garden on both sides of an immaculately trimmed yard. The garden was colorful and filled with roses, peonies, nicotiana, and huge digitalis plants. I was fortunately familiar with most of these flowers because of my grandmother's garden. Mrs. Rush had a bucket holding various garden tools including clippers, a garden shovel, and a hoe. She asked if I had any knowledge of flowering plants and I told her about my grandmother's garden. She was relieved and told me I was to pull weeds from the garden and then then to trim the bushes before sprinkling. She told me that arthritis now prevented her from doing much in the garden and was appreciative of the help.

It took me about two hours to weed both sides of the garden. I finished the trimming and started to sprinkle. I looked at my watch and realized that the whole job only took me a little over two hours to complete. Would I still get paid for four hours or would my pay correspond to the time worked? I knocked at the back door. She answered immediately, came out looked around the yard, and seemed satisfied.

"My dear," she said, "You must be exhausted, having worked all day."

"I got the job done in a little over two hours," I said.

"Wonderful! I'll call the office. You'll get your pay from them. Thanks for helping an old lady."

I smiled and walked back to the office, disappointed in my first real work experience.

The secretary of Manpower looked over the work sheet Mrs. Rush had filled out. Two and a half hours she had filled in, just as I told her.

"I'll get your paycheck. Wait there," she said, pointing to chairs along the wall.

My mind was thinking that working for Manpower was not the kind of job I was searching for and I needed to look through the classifieds again. It didn't take long for my name to be called and I was handed an envelope containing my wages. *At least I should get twelve fifty,* I thought.

Getting home, I told my mom about my initial work experience as I tore open the envelope. It took a while to recover from the shock of seeing that the check was not for twelve fifty but was only for eight dollars and forty-nine cents. Deducted from my check was social security tax, federal withholding tax, and a job finding fee from Manpower. I had never considered that there would be deductions. It was another day of learning about the real world. The real world wasn't sunshine and beach days.

My mother, sensing my discouragement, told me to apply for work at Waldameer Park. She needlessly reminded me of my attachment to the park and encouraged me to go there and find out what jobs were available.

"Don't fret about getting there. We'll take care of that for now and soon you'll be able to drive yourself. I think," she said, "we should go down to the motor vehicles office and have you apply for your learner's permit."

Immediately, my mood improved. Later that afternoon, just before the office was to close, I obtained my learner's permit at long last. My mother told me to get in the driver's seat. My driving lesson had now begun. If I made my mother nervous, she didn't show it.

"Try not to hug the right side so much," she said. "I think," she commented later, "you can go a little faster than fifteen miles an hour."

My black cloud had been lifted and my sun was shining brightly. I called Mike to share my good news and told him that I would be applying at Waldameer Park.

"I'll pick you up tomorrow at ten. Let's both apply. This will be great!" he added.

CHAPTER SIX

Right on time, Mike pulled up in his T-Bird. He was wearing, as was his usual style, a polo shirt and jeans. I decided to get a bit more dressed up. My prep school habits were hard to break. I wore a button-down dress shirt and a pair of blue slacks. I had even shined my shoes. It was important I thought to look good to make a good first impression.

"This is an amusement park," Mike commented. "It's not like you're applying at the First National Bank."

We arrived at the west parking lot. There were twenty cars or so in the lot. As we walked to the park office, we could see a great deal of bustle. The game building was alive with people who were busy cleaning, while others were stocking the shelves with the stuffed animals and other things that were the prizes for the games. The gift shop doors were wide open and the same thing was happening. A utility cart was parked in front of the Comet roller coaster and there were four guys loading the coaster's train with sandbags. Someone else had a pressure hose and was washing down the midway. A black Cadillac was parked in front of the office and two elderly ladies were busy planting petunias in the garden there.

The park was opening for the season on Saturday and preparations were underway for the big day. As we were about to enter the office, a man in a hurry exited, nodded a greeting in our direction, and headed into the park.

One of the ladies gardening commented that, "He never sits still enough to breath."

Two ladies were in the office. One was on the phone while the other, a youngish woman looked up from her desk in our direction. Briefly looking us over she asked if we were here to book the Union Bank picnic. Taken by surprise at the question, I mumbled that we were here to apply for jobs. She opened her desk drawer, pulled out two applications, and handed them to us, instructing us to be sure to fill out the complete paper.

Mike and I sat down and started to fill it in when the man who we saw earlier, returned to the office. He went to a desk, picked up his phone and made several phone calls. He got up from his desk, took the applications, looked them over. and told us to be here tomorrow at eleven.

I stupidly asked, "Does that mean I got the job?"

He didn't answer, but just nodded his head and said, "Be here tomorrow at eleven if you want to work here."

We were both excited and happy as we walked back to the car.

"Let's celebrate," said Mike.

We drove to my house and my mother was just as pleased as we were.

"What's the pay like?" my mom asked.

I stood there dumbfounded. We never even asked about it. We realized we knew nothing about our employment. We didn't know what we were going to be paid. We didn't know our hours or our schedules. We didn't even know what our jobs were going to be. All we knew was that we were going to be working at Waldameer Park.

Mike and I went to a tavern restaurant we liked. Despite the fact we weren't quite twenty-one, we started to go there recently because they served the best hamburgers in the city. We were both giddy with excitement as we downed our cheeseburgers, fries, and Cokes. Life was not just good. It was great!

Later that night, I stood looking out the back window towards the house that looked like the merry-go-round. I could see it spinning around and listening to the music, I saw myself working at Waldameer Park.

Mike was going to pick me up at nine forty-five. This would give us plenty of time to get there and look around. I was hoping we would have the opportunity to pick out what kind of job we would be assigned. The park had re-placed the old midway games building with a new steel structure. There would be a new area for the arcade games as well as six or seven traditional midway games. The doors to each of the new games were open and I could see there was a shooting gallery, a balloon game, a game with hoops, and a couple of others.

Several other guys and girls were arriving to learn their assignments and instructions for the jobs they would do. The man that we had met the previous day came out of the office accompanied by a thin, young man and walked over to the group. We learned that the young man was Don Morgan, who was the new games manager. They looked over the group and started to pull people out and send them to an assigned job. Mike got sent to a ball game at the end of the building. This was a game that required knocking down dolls by throwing a ball. If three dolls were knocked down off the shelf, the person would win a large stuffed animal. It was a simple game that would attract young men eager to impress their dates with their skill and strength.

There were only three of us left. The boss pointed and sent the remaining two, who were next to me, to the refreshment stand. Then he told me, the only remaining candidate, to go to the office and wait. He promised to be back shortly. I watched as he hurried around the park joined by a man wearing a shirt that said "superintendent" on the back. They walked up the ramp to the Comet roller coaster. The park was set to open for its seventieth season in a few minutes. People were starting to stream into the park with excited kids running to look at the rides and pick out what they wanted to on first.

As I sat in the office, I could hear that the merry-go-round music had started to play. The calliope sound of "The Sidewalks of New York" filled the air. I wanted desperately to be out there, assigned to any job. I anxiously waited. *Why didn't I get assigned?* I wondered. The boss came into the office said something to the ladies working there and disappeared again.

During his fourth charge into the office, I blurted out in a nervous sounding voice, "Do I have a job or not?"

He nodded his head and hustled out of the office again. *The man never sits still,* I thought.

The park was very crowded for so early in the season. I then remembered that the local pop music station was sponsoring a concert with the group Herman's Hermits. The group had a hit song "Henry the Eighth" that was in the top ten records for that week.

Suddenly, the boss came in and said, "Follow me."

He took me to the refreshment stand which was being overrun by customers waiting for their orders.

"He'll help you out today," the boss said to a gray haired, older man who was obviously the manager of the stand. "I don't have time to explain where everything is, but you look bright enough to figure things out," he said as he rushed off to the other end of the place.

"I want two large cokes and the extra large box of popcorn," said a blonde kid with an anxious face. "Can you hurry it up? I've got to get in line." he cried out.

I saw where the cups were kept and found the soda dispenser.

"So far so good," I said to myself.

Now to find the popcorn machine. I managed to find it in the opposite corner from where I was stationed. I filled the box and returned to the waiting young man.

"How much?" he asked.

I had no idea of the prices. The kid near me told me what the charges would be and saved me from panicking. The next two hours seemed to fly by as the refreshment stand was constantly bombarded with customers.

I saw the bus carrying the group depart, passing through the middle of the midway. Some of the band members were waving as they passed. The crowd of guests started to disperse. the midway was clearing. Some of the rides were still operating, but things had really calmed down. I finally was able to stand quiet as I wondered if this was to be my permanent work location. The manager of the stand walked over. He introduced himself to me.

"I'm Red and that's Helen, the grill master is my wife. You did a really good job considering your lack of preparation. Thanks a lot for helping. Torque said you are to return to the office. He'll see you there."

It seemed that I was not destined to work in the refreshment stand. What was my job assignment? Hopefully I'd find out soon.

"Take this to Don. He's probably in the arcade," said the boss, handing me an envelope. "Be here a little early tomorrow so we can train you to be working at the shooting gallery."

Wow! I finally knew where I was assigned. The park closed early that day. Mike and I had spent our first day as employees of Waldameer Park, even though I still had no idea of my assignment. It was the first day of the park's season and became part of my 'seasoning' on my life's journey.

CHAPTER SEVEN

A season at the Park ran from early May until Labor Day. My first unforgetta-ble season is ingrained in my heart and mind and is still part of who I am.

The shooting gallery was a new facility replacing an older one that used real weapons. The one I was operating used BBs instead of bullets. The targets were moving steel birds and mammals as well as targets. Customers would pay twenty-five cents for a tube full of BBs. My job was to fill the gun with the tube's contents and take the money. I was amazed how men especially were attracted to it in order usually to impress their wife or girlfriend with their macho strength and aim. Women seldom tried to shoot. My first day as an employee ended and I looked forward to the rest of the season.

Mike and I drove home, enthusiastic about our jobs. When I entered my home, my mom was anxious to hear all about it.

"Did you find out what you'll be paid?" my mother asked.

I still didn't know. To me, the job was more important than my pay. I knew that payday would be a surprise.

Busy days had me constantly active. We had eight guns and it was a chal-lenge to fill the guns and keep things moving. Other days, however, were much quieter. On those days I would stand at the booth and observe the go-ings on throughout the park. The gallery was directly across from the merry-go-round which was next to the Comet roller coaster. On the one side of me was the bumper cars and on the other side was the penny arcade. In between the games and bumper cars was a ticket booth. This section of the park usually was the busiest even on quiet days. There seemed to be people always in the arcade playing skee-ball or one of the pinball machines.

I started to wander over to the ticket booth and talk to the cashier. Her name was Elsa and she had worked at the Park for over fifty years. I was mesmerized by her tales of what the park was like in its early days. She told me about the original coaster, the RavineFlyer. She had been a cashier the day of the accident that would eventually lead to its demise. She had been there when a fire destroyed the park's "Hofbrau" theater restaurant. This was a restaurant bar that served German food and plenty of beer while guests would sing along with the band. It also usually had entertainment like a singer or comedian. The Hofbrau had been a lively place to go. Elsa had so many stories that made quiet days go by quickly.

The boss was constantly on the move. He would walk up and down, supervising the midway, making sure everything was in order. Nothing escaped his attention. On those rare days when the park was very quiet, and the boss was tied up in his office, some of us guys would ride the bumper cars or make their way to the Comet to steal a quick ride. Working at an amusement park could be a lot of fun.

I had never been on the Comet. It wasn't a behemoth of a coaster and yet the idea of riding a vehicle over which a person had no control was intimidating.

"Come on, the park's empty. Ray will give us a ride on the Comet," one of the guys yelled.

Mike had left his stand and was eager for a ride.

"Hurry," said Mike, "the boss left the park and Don is probably eating somewhere."

I stood there petrified. There was no way I could back out short of fainting on the spot.

"Okay," I mumbled.

Sometimes things a person fears turns out to be nothing. The ride is considered a classic junior roller coaster. It was great fun and best of all, I had conquered an irrational fear. I wanted a shirt that said "I survived the Comet."

My first day as an employee of the park was memorable. The first three weeks were very busy. It was school picnic season. Every day there would be two or three different schools and the park would be filled with kids, their parents, and their teachers. You would see nuns in their habits and veils lined up to ride the skyrocket or the bumper cars or any one of the other rides. Sisters walked about holding cotton candy or candy apples. I never had any sister at my shooting gallery though.

On some days before Mike would pick me up, my mom and I would go for a driving lesson. She would have me drive her to the market or have me try to parallel park on a busy street. I was gaining confidence behind the wheel and was anxiously looking forward to taking my driver's test.

Elsa and I often squeezed in a little time to chat. She had a special needs daughter who lived with her and often accompanied her to work. Evie, the daughter, would sit on a bench near the ticket booth and seemed to relish people watching. Elsa was in her eighties and Evie was probably near sixty. She told me she worried about what would become of Evie when she passed. Of course, she would add, that would not be for many years. I loved that she always looked forward and, even while reminiscing about the past, believed the best is yet to come.

One day as I walked to say hello to her, I saw her take a couple dollars out of her wallet and put it in the till. She told me that a previous guest earlier that day was accidentally undercharged for his tickets. Realizing her error, she was making up the difference out of her own money.

"I couldn't sleep tonight if I let that go," she said.

Mike told me that Jill's mother was working full time to put a distance between the two of them. Jill was going away to visit relatives in California and would be away for several weeks. In August, she would be leaving for college. She would be going to Ohio State. Mike was going to attend St. Mark's so they would not be able to see each other for quite a while. Their relationship was in trouble.

My love life, as limited as it was previously, was now non-existent. Working all day, there was no opportunity to meet anyone. The park, once school picnic season ended, would be open from two until eleven or even later occasionally. It was open seven days a week. Days off were usually spent with necessary tasks that couldn't be done while working.

I received a letter from the college that it was time to schedule an appointment to declare my major and arrange the schedule for my classes. I set the date for the following week. It was now time for me to finally decide on a college major. One thing was certain, it was not going to be calculus.

The other important thing in my life was taking my driver's test.

"Let's go for it," I told my mom.

We decided to do it the same day as my meeting at the college. And to think that I originally planned that as the day I would finally get a haircut! I guess that would have to be postponed for another time.

CHAPTER EIGHT

My appointment at Gannon was for nine-thirty. My mother waited patiently as I entered the office of the guidance director. All week I had agonized over selecting a major for my course of studies at the university. My high school grades did not give me much information except to steer me away from engineering and anything requiring an aptitude for math. I considered psychology or perhaps sociology, except that my heart just wasn't into studying those areas. In the middle of the previous night, a revelation came to me. Political science would be my major. I have often considered becoming a lawyer and poli-sci was really pre-law. The councilor and I planned my course of study for the coming semester. My imagination saw me as a congressman or maybe even a senator!

After almost two hours at Gannon, it was time for D-Day, my driving test. With great apprehension, I entered the queue for the test. My mother left the car to sit in the waiting room. I thought I saw her holding her rosary beads as she walked toward it. There were about six cars in front of me. I watched as a state police officer entered the first car, put on the seatbelt, and directed the would-be driver to enter the course. It looked pretty basic with a straight road, curves, a stop sign, a four-way intersection, and a stop light. The challenge was parallel parking. According to the driver's manual, it should only require three movements to park in between two other vehicles. The young lady I was watching took six. There was a lot of weeping as the officer indicated that she had failed to pass. Of the following five cars, three had been successful and two others had failed. It was now my turn.

Quickly, an officer opened the door to sit next to me. I handed him my credentials, an ID, and my learner's permit. He looked them over and directed me to begin driving the course. I was driving my mother's 1962 Plymouth Savoy. It was a stripped-down car, not even having a radio.

"Not necessary," my mother would say. "A radio would just use up the battery faster. I don't need music when I drive."

Slowly, I started to drive. My hands were sweaty as I clutched the steering wheel. I don't think I ever went faster than twenty miles an hour, but I was confident I met all the necessary requirements. The last test was the parallel parking. I pulled forward aligning myself with the car in front, looked back as I turned the wheel thinking to myself, "Don't hit the curb!" The car slid into place, as I pulled forward. Three movements! The only question was whether I was close enough to the curb. I waited as the officer opened his door to see. He handed me back my papers and directed that I go into the office to obtain my temporary license. I had passed!

My mother and dad were both pleased but reminded me that there were now four drivers for two cars. My older brother was finishing college and working part time at a bank. The Plymouth my mother drove was my grandparents' vehicle. My grandfather, however, was not able to drive anymore so it was now my mother's job to drive him to his job at the toy factory. My dad, of course, needed his car for work every day. I was now a legitimate, fully licensed driver in the state of Pennsylvania. Things were looking up.

With the conclusion of school picnics, the park was now quiet during weekday afternoons. Idleness led to a little wandering. Occasionally, some of the guys would ride the Comet. We reasoned that the track needed to be warmed up to keep up the speed of the coaster train. Sometimes we would play some of the machines in the arcade. I became pretty good at skee-ball, but when I used up all my nickels, it was time to stop. Elsa and I would chat about everything. Sometimes Ray, the merry-go-round operator would join us. I learned a lot about them both and came to enjoy their companionship.

Ray reminded me of Edward G. Robinson, the actor. He was short and stocky with a face that was well traveled. Some of the other guys regarded him as an old grump. Initially, one would think that. Whenever possible, he was smoking cigarettes, cigars, or sometimes even a pipe. He had worked at the park off and on for many years. He lived in a nearby beach cottage. He told me that over the years he had operated every attraction at the park and was especially fond of running the Comet. Ray looked grumpy but was pretty soft-spoken with a hint of kindness hidden in a rough exterior. He loved being a ride operator and was extremely conscientious about his job. Every day he would arrive early carrying a lunch box and a thermos of hot coffee, set them down in the engine room, and proceed to meticulously go over the ride. He would walk touching each of the animals in the carved menagerie, making sure they were clean and ready to go for the day.

"The other day I found the elephant seating area was sticky from cotton candy," he told me one day.

He wanted and expected that everything be perfect on his merry-go-round. Ray's attitude reminded me that no matter what the job entailed it should be carried out with pride and dignity. This was a lesson that I would carry throughout my entire life. After working at the park a couple of weeks, I began to appreciate the characters who populated the workforce. It was easy to deduce that none of the regular staff had every had the opportunity to attend a prep school. None of them was looking forward to beginning college in the fall and certainly none aspired to become a lawyer. Yet there were a lot of things to learn from them and that included good and bad things and for a naive kid like me it would shape my entire life.

My Catholic school upbringing was responsible for my purity of language. Sure, I heard some of my fellow prepsters use all the colorful vernacular words that are very common today. However, I just couldn't. Other guys, including Mike, sometimes would use words describing male or female anatomy in speaking of someone that had somehow offended them. I would listen, but even though I might have felt upset or angry, my mouth would never use those words. At home, the most words of anger were "son of a b" or "damn it". Pretty tame stuff by today's standards.

My inhibitions towards using colorful language eventually melted away as a result of working with this motley and colorful crew. I never had experienced hearing such colorful descriptions of a broken piece of equipment. The broken gear was a "f...ing piece of sh..." that would require a "f...ing whole f...ing day" to replace. It was a real "c ...cksucker". Butch, the park superintendent, a great guy, used the most colorful language in describing anything that was broken and needed replacement. Almost all the other guys had similar vocabularies and, when not in the earshot of guests, would let go a stream of profanities that was almost strangely poetic and in fact, as I came to see, described the situation accurately.

Mr. Nielson and Butch came one morning to the gallery to ask me if I wanted another assignment. I enthusiastically said yes. They wanted me to be a ride operator. I was going to be trained to run a ride called the Flying Coaster. It was a circular ride with the cars going over a small incline flying and then landing on the track to repeat the circle. It was considered a thrill ride because of its high speed. It was one of the most popular rides at Waldameer Park.

This was not a typical push a button, run the ride kind of operation. The operator would have to focus on a car, turn off the control at a particular place and guide this vehicle around the track and over the hill to bring the ride to a stop. Butch and another of the maintenance staff spent the entire day training me in the ride's operation. The first few times I tried to bring the ride to a stop, I often misjudged the distance and would have the control vehicle miss going over the hill or have the vehicle go too far past the intended stopping point. By the end of the day, I was successfully maneuvering the designated car over the hill into its targeted location. I had become the operator of the Flying Coaster!

The park closed at ten that night and Mike and I decided to stop at McDonald's for a celebratory cheeseburger and fries. Mike told me that he and Jill were no longer going together. Jill was away for the remainder of the summer and was off to college immediately following. He was devastated. They had been together a couple of years and he was not prepared for the abrupt end of their relationship. For me, this McDonald's trip was to celebrate, but for Mike it was a wake.

CHAPTER NINE

It was my first day as the ride operator of the second most popular ride at Waldameer Park, the Flying Coaster. It was a picnic day which meant that the park would soon be crowded with kids and adults eager to take a spin on the Flying Coaster. I eagerly looked forward to a busy, exciting day. The early part of the day met all my expectations. I had a long line of guests waiting for their turn. The ride itself had ten cars each attached by an arm from the center motor. Usually that meant at least twenty or more guests could be accommodated each time. The line waiting to get on had at least forty guests and was growing as the crowd increased through the afternoon. Looking out towards the midway, I could see crowds of people walking holding candy apples or other park goodies. There were kids running eagerly from ride to ride and along with the music from the merry-go-round one could hear the screams of delight as they enjoyed the thrill each ride gave.

The Flying Coaster was located at the far end of the park a good distance from the location of the shooting gallery. Nearby was another ticket booth in front and two additional rides to the right. The Flying Scooter was a standard amusement park attraction that allowed the rider to control the flight of a vehicle by turning a flap up or down. Next to it was the ride very common to all parks, the Tilt-a-Whirl. This was a circular ride with small hills on which a vehicle would be able to make a complete revolution.

Herb was the operator of the Tilt and another man called Bud ran the scooter planes. In the nearby ticket booth sat Lou. Lou, a lady in her early eighties, had worked at the park for thirty years. She needed employment after her husband had died. She had been working there every summer since. Like Elsa, she was a gem. She loved the park and even in her old age she would eagerly look forward to the summer season. Elsa and Lou both would work at the ballroom during the park's off-season. Lou had retired from working the ballroom in the winter now working only for the summer. I was impressed by this team of cashiers who were honest and reliable. They never called in sick, working every day that they were scheduled. They loved their jobs and always had positive, cheerful interactions with the guests.

The following day I was feeling comfortable and excited about being a ride operator. The schedule for the day indicated that it was to be another busy day with many picnics happening. I chatted a bit with my ride neighbors, Herb and Bud, before heading to my ride to ready it for the day. One of the first responsibilities was to remove the canvas covers from each of the cars. Then I was to check that the area around the ride was swept clean. I walked around the ride checking the safety bars and looked to make sure the seats were clean. All was well. The Flying Coaster was ready to receive guests.

The crowd in the midway was growing. Eager kids and adults started to line up for the first ride of the day. At exactly one o'clock, I opened the gate, took the tickets, and filled every seat on the ride. I started the motor and slowly opened the valve that initiated movement on the ride. It reached speed and was merrily spinning and flying as it was supposed to do. I did notice, however, that it sounded different. There seemed to be a bit of a squeaky noise from the motor that I had not noticed before. It completed the twenty cycles as intended. The passengers were discharged. I went to the entrance gate to load up for the next group. The ride ran as before, but the squeaky sound persisted and even seemed louder. This continued for the next few ride cycles. I started to believe the noise was nothing to worry about. I would ask the ride super about it when the opportunity presented itself.

Late in the afternoon, it happened. The ride screamed a loud yell and suddenly started to slow down. There was no way to choose the designated car to go over the hill. I let the ride go until a car passed over and then I applied the brake before letting it drift back into position. It was a bumpy ride for the guests. I indicated to them to exit their seats. A few wanted to know when the ride would restart. A few of them grumbled about the rough end and the shortened ride. The line, meanwhile, stayed in place. I explained that we were closed until further notice. After the area was cleared of guests, I ran to the office to report the breakdown.

Over the loudspeaker came the call, "Butch and Mr. Nielson go to the Flying Coaster."

I went back to my position and waited. I could see the boss briskly walking in the middle of the midway headed in my direction. It wasn't long before the utility vehicle carrying Butch and his assistant Ronnie arrived.

"What the hell happened?" asked Butch, looking at me.

I explained about the squeaky sound and the sudden screech that happened later.

My descriptive vocabulary was enhanced in ways I never imagined as Butch looked at the motor in the center of the ride. The most uncensored thing that he said was "It's the chain."

It took about two hours for Butch and Ron to get the chain back together and on its track. They ran the ride three or four times to check it. The squeaky sound was gone. I could reopen the Flying Coaster. It didn't take long to fill all the seats. It was ready to go. I started the engine with a slight feeling of trepidation. It started to move and soon was at full speed flying over the bump. All seemed well. A line started to form of eager guests ready to ride. Closing time came. I put the covers over all the cars, turned off the lights, pulled the power switch and was relieved that everything was back to normal.

On the way home, Mike continued brooding about his breakup with Jill. I reassured him that as the saying goes, "There are other fish in the sea." My little pep talk only elicited an icy stare.

"Same time tomorrow," he said as I exited the car.

I arrived at the park early, hoping to run it a couple of times to make sure everything was alright. I took the covers off and walked around it as I checked that the area was clean and ready for the day. All the while, I was saying a silent prayer as I turned it on to see it do its thing. The rides were tested daily before opening by the park mechanics, but today I wanted to see for myself that all was in order.

Today promised a light schedule with only two small picnics scheduled. Everything was ready and at one o'clock the Flying Coaster was ready to soar! At two-thirty it happened. The workings of the ride seemed to be in complete revolution. The ride came to a stop. I could see the chain detached from the cogs that made it operational. I ran once again to the office to report what happened. Mr. Nielson was at his desk, looked up, and instinctively knew something was terribly wrong. As we walked together back to the ride, I kept apologizing for somehow breaking it. I was holding myself responsible. He didn't say anything, just gave me a perplexed stare.

Butch and the maintenance crew arrived. Then I heard a barrage of colorful adjectives applied to the mechanical center of the ride with new and unconventional descriptions that I never learned from Sister Catherine in English class. It was eventually decided that it would require more than just typical maintenance. It needed a complete overhaul that included a new chain, new drive belts, and perhaps a new engine. My ride would be closed for a while.

"I'm sorry, I'm sorry!" I kept repeating. "Maybe I should be reassigned back to the shooting gallery or perhaps to games."

I was told to go to the kid's ride section and help Leo and Justin who were the ride operators there.

The kiddie section was designed for the riding experiences for toddlers and other young children. It included a boat ride, pony and cart ride, firetrucks, a rocket ride that ascended a couple of feet, a ride that the kids had to turn a wheel to make it move, and the Cadillac ride. This was a car that ran on a track. Kids loved to pretend they were driving as they held on to a decorative steering wheel while the Cadillac car made its way around the track.

Leo was a well-dressed man in his fifties. He was the father of the Gypsy family that worked at the park. His wife and daughter had a tent on the midway where they told fortunes by palm reading. Their boys occasionally worked at the park. Many people referred to them as "gypsies" which is considered derogatory today. The Roma people were originally from India. They live on every continent, but especially in eastern Europe. Whatever name you would apply to them, they were exotic. They dressed differently, spoke differently, and just had an air of mystery about them. Often, they are regarded as undesirable vagrants or worse.

Justin, the other man in that section, was a big elderly man who spoke limited English. He looked strong and primarily operated the Cadillac cars. The cars would often get off track, but Justin was always there to lift them back on to keep his cars going. Justin was Russian. He had escaped communism and settled in the Erie because there was a sizable Russian presence in the city.

Leo was appreciative of my being assigned to help there. He showed me how the rides operated, which was very simple. Put the kids in the vehicle, or let the parent do it, then make sure the safety belt was attached. Push the button to start the ride and be close by to supervise its operation.

I walked over to Justin and spoke Polish to him. His eyes lit up and he gave me a hug. Polish and Russian share some words in common and the languages are compatible. Justin and I would often chat and seemed to feel less isolated because he now had someone he could communicate with, even though my Polish was limited.

"Dziekuja! Dziekuja!", "Thank you, thank you!" he would say, appreciating my feeble attempt at communicating using my Polish to translate his Russian into English.

During that season, I often spent time with my new friends, a Roma family and a Russian emigree. It occurred to me that despite the great differences in culture and language, there was a common humanity that enriched my life with a kaleidoscope of wonder.

My ego was still bruised. Had I somehow been responsible for the calamity of having to temporarily close one of the major park attractions? It took four days for the ride to be repaired That morning as I reported for work, Mr. Nielson told me to go back to the Flying Coaster. I had not been reassigned. My plea to go back to the shooting gallery had been ignored. I guess it wasn't my fault. The Flying Coaster continued to soar unimpeded by mechanical breakdowns the rest of that summer.

Summer was flying by, headed towards just becoming a memory and the season's end was in sight. Orientation Day at the college was scheduled for August eighteenth. On this day, the new freshmen class would be shown around the campus and given a preview of college life. This was the first year the college was admitting women having previously been an all-male college. I informed the park office that I would not be able to work that date. I was about to enter a new phase of my life.

Mike was still brooding. He was preoccupied with the idea that Jill's rejection was a cataclysmic sign of failure. My dating life was essentially non-existent. I loved my job. I loved working at Waldameer and didn't have time for anything else.

Butch and Mr. Nielson headed toward me one afternoon with a serious expression that I interpreted as if I did something wrong. The only thing I could think of was that one night I had failed to put the canvas covers over the cars and unfortunately it had rained during the night, making the seats a little soggy. I had worked diligently the following morning to wipe the seats and dry them off as best as I was able.

"I'm sorry about forgetting to put the covers on the other night" I blurted out as they approached.

"Huh?" said Mr. Nielson in a puzzled tone of voice. "We need someone to be the ride operator for the Comet. Ray will train you and stay with you there for a few days. You'll start tomorrow."

In my mind, this was the equivalent of winning the lottery. The Comet was the park's only roller coaster and was the most popular ride at the park. It was confirmation that they liked what I did and were willing to trust me with the most prestigious ride position. I was elated!

CHAPTER TEN

I told Mike that would drive that day. My mother had no plans to shop, so the car would be free. This didn't happen very often, so it was a real red-letter day. Mike said he would drive himself because he did not want to arrive that early. I left an hour early full of joyful anticipation. This was a super red-letter day.

I was early. There were only a couple of cars in the employee parking area. The office secretaries, Helen and Monica, started at nine each day and left at five most days. Mr. Nielson's mother also helped in the office most days. She lived in the park with Mrs. Mueller, the park owner. Mr. Nielson called her Aunt Hazel. Herb told me that he had been adopted by the Muellers who were childless and had promised the Nielsons that their son would inherit the park in this way, making the inheritance free of any obstacles.

Helen and Monica were great supports who were always ready to help with any issue that arose. They had a challenging job dealing with the employees, the suppliers, the guests, and even Mr. Nielson. They always performed their job with a positive, confident attitude.

I checked in that office and greeted them before racing to the ramp leading to the Comet. There it was sitting silently waiting for the start of a day that would involve many ups and downs for it. The red train was in the operating position with the blue train parked in the stationary position. On most days, only one train was used. Instinctively, I took a broom and started to sweep the platform. It was very clean as it was, but I needed something to do as I waited for Ray or Butch to come and get things started. Roller coasters need to be warmed up each morning by running the track several times before the guests arrived. The train would increase in speed as the day went by and it was important to test it out as well as to warm the tracks. I waited anxiously.

Ray had arrived. He carried his traditional lunch bucket and thermos of coffee which he sat down on a small table near the control lever. He reached in his pocket and put down two packs of Raleigh cigarettes, two Phillies cigars, a pipe and a can of Prince Albert tobacco. Ray always came prepared. I had never smoked and was sort of stunned at the abundance of smoking material he had brought with him.

He looked at me and said, "Let's get started. You can walk the track this morning."

At first, I didn't quite understand what he was saying. What did he mean by walk the track? At that moment, Butch and Mr. Nielson appeared.

"Ray will teach you all you'll need to know. We'll see you after you walk the track to get started running the train."

I am afraid of heights. You already know of my fear of water and now another of my phobias has been laid bare. The Comet was not a giant coaster, but the first hill was probably as tall as a three-story building. There was a board that ran next to the track with a guardrail to hold on to as you walked the track. Ray told me that the purpose of doing this each morning was to ensure that the track was free of branches from the many trees that surrounded it. Ray suggested that it was easier if you started at the end of the ride, a straight area preceded by three "bunny hop" hills before reaching the curve. From there a few more small hills led to an uphill climb to the next level. Around the next curve and then came the big hill followed by the main lead hill with the drive chain.

My first reaction was panic. The thought of having to climb the hills shook me to the core. After a few silent prayers, I clenched my teeth and started out on my journey.

I could see Ray lighting up his first cigarette of the morning and heard him say, "Hurry because we got to test it too and we ain't got all day!"

This part of walking the track was easy. The dips and climbs were not intimidating. I rounded the curve and looked down the straightaway with its slightly bigger dips and feeling more confident picked up my pace. There it was in front of me, the first real challenge. It was a climb that was on top of the coaster's house. The entrance to the Comet was right below. It was steep, but still manageable as I gritted my teeth grasping the handrail and ascended to the top. I dared to look down towards the midway and saw Mr. Nielson and Butch standing there looking up at me. They waved. "Hurry." I heard.

So far, so good. I hadn't embarrassed myself. I hadn't fallen and either killed or injured myself. *Hold on and keep moving,* I thought to myself. There it was the big hill. The Comet was unusual in that the second hill was bigger than the first drop and was more intimidating. Holding on, I climbed the hill then proceeded the downslope. I was almost there the lift hill stood in front of me almost glaring. Is this how Sir Edward Hillary felt facing the peak of Mt. Everest? Holding on for dear life, I reached the summit and started my expedition down. Ray on his third or fourth cigarette and Raleigh was waiting.

"You okay?" Ray asked. "Hey, do you need a smoke?"

"I think I do," I replied as I took my first cigarette from his pack and began a very bad habit that took me twenty years to conquer.

Butch, Mr. Nielson, and Ronnie the assistant mechanic climbed in as Ray turned on the lift chain and then released the brake.

"Watch me," he said. "I want you to do this for the next practice run."

He then moved to the other side of the control area to the brake handles. The Comet made its first run and as it approached the station, Ray moved the levers, slowing it down, and then stretched the lever completely open to bring the train to a safe stop right where it started from. Releasing the brake, he moved the cars forward to the loading area.

"Your turn," he said, pointing to the release lever.

We had three or four more practice runs. Butch and Mr. Nielson left leaving Ray and I to continue running the cars. Guests started to arrive. I could see Elsa in her ticket booth with a queue of excited kids clamoring for the chance to get on the rides. The Comet was ready. Ray was a good teacher. He was patient and taught me the operation of the brake system. My confidence grew as I took over running the number one ride at Waldameer Park.

The rest of that season I would repeat the walk. Neither rain, sleet, or snow could keep me from my appointed rounds. Snow in the middle of summer usually started in early July and would last two or three weeks of heavy flurries. Gem City weather can be unpredictable, but this snow is from the cottonwood trees that surrounded the park. The trees were very common in this area along the lakeshore. They would release their cotton like seed pods by the millions covering every surface with summer snow. The "snow" however, never slowed the Comet down.

CHAPTER ELEVEN

When I had free time, I would sometimes wander into the arcade to either buy my pack of Marlboros or to play one of the pinball machines. The cashier there was named Nevada. She and her daughter Ruth had worked at the park for several seasons. Ruth, a college student from the University of Chicago, worked at the park during her summer vacations. She worked in the office and did breaks for the cashiers in the park. Ruth was tall, very tall. She was probably about six feet tall, slim, and attractive in a traditional way. She was also very smart. A scholarship student, she was majoring in chemistry. Besides these attributes, she was a lot of fun with a good sense of humor that lit up any room.

Ruth, Mike, and I would often go out together after the park closed. We would get something to eat at McDonald's and sit in the parking lot talking and laughing about anything and everything. Ruth's mother was, we discovered, a Native American. She was a member of an obscure, small tribe related to the Eriez nation. Mike and I developed a relationship with Nevada when on our days off we would often spend time at Ruth's house playing cards. Nevada made it a foursome. Mike and I would pair against Ruth and her mom in pinochle. We became good at the game and while playing, solved all the problems of the world.

One day, Leo came up the ramp to the Comet.

"We are having a celebration in the round picnic shelter in honor of the feast of the Assumption. We are hoping that you can come and eat with us on this special feast day."

On August fifteenth, the feast of the Assumption, Leo and his clan would gather to celebrate the holy day by cooking a pig on a spit and enjoying each other's company.

The day of the feast, during my lunch break, I went to the round picnic shelter. There were probably over fifty people there. The women, like Mary, were probably all fortune tellers from other parks in nearby Ohio or New York. The men stopped talking and stared as I approached. Leo came up to me and with a big smile led me into the picnic area. The men relaxed and nodded hello. They were very kind and made sure that I had plenty to eat and drink. It was an amazing feast. A large tapestry hung in a corner and men and women would cross themselves as they stood in front of it. Mary was concerned that I was so thin.

"Eat more, eat more! You are too skinny," she said.

I returned to my position at the Comet with a sense of joy that I, an outsider to the Roma, had been invited to join them in their festive celebration.

The world is made up of many diverse and wonderful people. Most are just like us sharing the same values of love and family. The Roma may appear exotic and are often persecuted and ridiculed for looking a little bit different. Humanity is a colorful mosaic of wonder and beauty. I was blessed to have known them.

Mike was continuing his despondence over losing Jill. I thought he might be interested in dating Ruth. However, he regarded her as a close friend rather than a girlfriend. One evening on our way home, he told me he was going to quit work. He said he needed a "vacation" before starting college. I was surprised because in my mind working at Waldameer Park and our friendships there was like a vacation.

A couple of days later, his last day of working at the park, he wanted to celebrate. Ruth and I expected to go to one of our usual hangouts for burgers and cokes. Instead, Mike drove past them all and got on the interstate headed to New York state.

"Where are we going?" I asked.

He said he had heard of this great bar not far from the border between the states that served great food and lots of beer. New York state had a drinking age of eighteen. I had never considered going there to drink. My cautious conscience reminded me of fatal accidents that had occurred when kids our age went to establishments along the border to drink. This would be a first for me, but not for Ruth who enthusiastically approved the plan.

The bar was a non-descript brick building with a small neon sign on the roof that blinked 'The Hideaway'. There were many cars with Pennsylvania plates in the parking lot, indicating to me that going here was not an original idea. We picked a booth in the corner away from a noisy group of mostly young men laughing and shouting. The dimly lit bar was also filled with the music from the nearby jukebox playing Connie Francis singing "v-a-c-a-t-i-o-n, in the summertime".

Mike went to the bar and came back with three beers. I had tasted beer at home when my dad would give me just a sip from his bottle. Beer was not anything I craved. In fact, it tasted terrible. However, under the circumstances, I started to drink it. A waitress came over and asked if we wanted anything to eat. Mike looked at the menu and pointed out that on the back side it listed in alphabetical order all kinds of mixed drinks the bar served.

"Let's start with the A drink and see how far down the list we can get," Mike yelled.

Ruth enthusiastically agreed.

I thought to myself, *What have I got myself into?*

Mike ordered Amaretto Sours for all of us. They went down easily and tasted great. Next, he ordered a drink called a Bellini, followed by a Black Russian, a Bloody Mary, and a Brandy Alexander. I lost track of the names of the next two drinks. I got up from our table wanting to go to the bathroom. It was like walking on the merry-go-round. The room was going round and round. I made it to the urinal, but my aim was off. I kept thinking I needed to apologize to someone for peeing on their floor.

Mike came in, put his hand around me, and said, "We're going home now!"

Ruth drove. She seemed totally non-affected by consuming all these drinks while Mike and I were messed up. I more so than Mike.

Arriving in front of my house, I could hear Mike and Ruth whispering to each other. The light was on in the hall, indicating that my mom was awake and waiting for me to get home. She always waited up. The discussion between Mike and Ruth concerned how they were going to get me into the house and past my mom without her knowing I was totally soused. They led me to the front door, cautioning me to walk in, say goodnight, and head for the bathroom. Hopefully, my mom would go to bed then and I could get to my bedroom without incident.

Mike walked me up the stairs, straightened out my shirt, and whispered to himself, "Here goes nothing."

"Hi," he said cheerfully to my mom.

I nodded to her and carefully step by step made my way to the bathroom.

"He's tired having had a long, hard day at the park. I'll be seeing you," he said. "Dan's probably anxious to get to bed. It was an exciting day."

I came out of the bathroom, smiled at my mom, and managed to get in the bedroom without falling. Mike, relieved, said good night and left.

Somehow, I had succeeded. Either my mother never realized how drunk I was that night, or she never let on that she ever knew. Mike and I worked on that alphabetical list often during the next year. We never drank more than two drinks each time, so it was never like that first time. I guess you could call me an experienced drinker now.

CHAPTER TWELVE

I missed seeing Mike every day since he was no longer working at the park. Most days I was able to drive my mom's car but there were days she would have to drive me back and forth. I really wished I had a car and would not need to depend on her for my transportation.

I started to eat lunch with Herb. He was a middle-aged, unassuming man from Franklin, Pa. This was a small town about a hundred miles away. He would come every summer to work at the park running the Tilt-a-whirl. He wasn't married and resided with his sister in Franklin. I came to know him as an uncomplicated, plain-speaking guy satisfied with a quiet, simple life. He was always calm and happy, no matter the circumstances.

Joining us for lunch occasionally was Matt. He worked at the balloon game, was the same age as me and, while being very affable, also had a serious side. Before eating lunch, he would bow his head and say grace. Even with my Catholic schooling, I was surprised. One lunch, he told me that come September he would be studying for the priesthood at a seminary in Michigan. This was a complete surprise. Matt becoming Father Matt! Waldameer was home to a diverse group of employees.

Running the Comet had its advantages over running the other rides. A roller coaster is the prestige ride of any park. It is the most visible as well as the most popular. While the Comet wasn't very big, it still fit the bill. One of the advantages had to do with girls! Often girls would hang around the ramp and want to chat. I felt very macho smoking a Marlboro while running the coaster. The girls were very good at flirting while at the same time aiming to convince me to give them a free ride. I admit to occasionally being bewitched and giving in to their feminine charms. I'm not sure we males have any defense when girls launch their offense against us defenseless young men.

Every couple of days, a group of five or six girls in their late teens or early twenties would come to the park. They all were knockouts. They were full of charm and very friendly. The Comet was their favorite ride. One of the girls, a petite blonde, introduced herself. Jenny was from Pittsburgh. I asked whether she was a student at one of the local colleges. She responded that she was in business and worked out of the Hideaway Hotel. I wondered what kind of business this girl was doing, imagining her in the beauty industry or perhaps working as a model. She was always very friendly and had a winning sense of humor. She was a little older than I was, but I thought about asking her to go out for something to eat after the park closed.

Every morning I browsed through the *Erie Daily Times* to keep up to the local news. This one morning looking over the section for local news was the headline: PROSTITUTE RING BROKEN. Reading further the story said that a group of professional prostitutes were arrested working out of the Hideaway Hotel. My girls were hookers. My shock turned to sorrow when I thought about these beautiful, charming young ladies working in this way. Why someone so attractive, personable, intelligent, and witty would do this is something I will never understand. This was another blow to my naivety, my seasoning for the world.

Summer was rapidly coming to a close. The hot temperatures were giving way to cooler temperatures. Change was in the air but there were still a few big days ahead. Park attendance was kept up by several big picnics. The biggest picnic of the year was the General Electric union picnic that brought several thousand people to the park for a day in late August. Butch and the maintenance staff worked especially hard to ensure that all the rides were in tip-top shape for the big day.

College orientation day arrived. I dressed in a button-down blue shirt with newly pressed slacks that my mom insisted I wear, telling me that, "when you look good, you feel good." It also makes a good impression. I was used to wearing a dress shirt and tie from my years at Prep. We even wore a blazer with the school insignia sewn on the front. Prep boys, it was hoped, would become men of distinction. At Gannon, there was no dress requirement, but my mother insisted I not forget the sartorial lessons learned at Prep.

All the freshmen and women were given beanies to wear. An upper-class student from each department would be our mentor and guide for the tour. My department, political science, was centered on the second floor of the humanities building. The department head was a priest who had escaped from the Russian occupation of Lithuania. Dr. Burr had been a professor at the Catholic university there before the Russian invasion of his country. Meeting him, I was impressed by his intelligence and strength of character. I liked him immediately and looked forward to my studies there. The rest of the tour we were shown other buildings and were given a good introduction to college life. I looked forward to a new phase of my life.

The day of the GE picnic arrived. Butch and Mr. Nielson came up the ramp to get the second train put on the track. Two trains would be running on the Comet that day. Ray came up the ramp soon after loaded down with the usual thermos, lunch bucket and pockets full of smoking material. Two trains made things more complicated when running the coaster. Two operators were helpful in keeping things safe. I took the front brake where guests were admitted and seated. My job was to fill the seats, check to make sure the lap bar was secure, and when the second train arrived in the station, I would release the train for its run.

The park was filled to overflowing. There was a long line that stretched across the midway for the Comet. Everyone was given a box of Cracker Jack when they checked in at the Union's desk. By that evening, when the picnic ended, Ray and I looked out to see the midway knee deep in Cracker Jack boxes. Ray and I lit up a smoke, shook hands, and smiled. He walked down the ramp and exited my life, becoming one of the Waldameer Park personalities that became engraved in my mind.

CHAPTER THIRTEEN

It rained on Labor Day. The last day of the season started with dark gray clouds that symbolized my feelings about the end. It was so dark that some of the rides were lit up as if it were night. A few people had ventured out, seemingly oblivious to the rain, perhaps hoping to get one more ride on the Comet. Some people were hoping to enjoy their last candy apple or perhaps they enjoyed cotton candy. It might be eight months before they were able to get these tastes of summer again. Winter in Erie was often harsh and unrelenting. Snow would frequently be on the ground from about Halloween to Easter. Bleak skies became the norm. It was as if the sun had fled to Florida.

I stood on the Comet platform looking out towards the midway. I saw Elsa in her ticket booth while Evie was sitting on a stool in the nearby arcade. There was Lou, the cashier, on the other side of the park. Barely visible from my position was Nevada in the change booth in the arcade. Mary was sitting on a chair in the fortune teller's tent smoking a cigarette and waiting for someone seeking to have their fortune read. Leo would sometimes walk from his position in nearby Kiddieland to talk to her. Ruth, Nevada's daughter, would occasionally come out of the office to check on the cashiers. Herb and Bud were standing under the cover of the refreshment stand, chatting with Red the manager and Helen, his wife. Butch and Ronnie zipped by on the utility vehicle and headed to the arcade. They parked it by Elsa's booth and went into the arcade probably, I speculated, to get a pack of smokes.

A couple of teenagers soaked to the skin dashed up the ramp laughing and enjoying the rain that was steadily falling.

"You open?" the tall, lanky boy shouted out to me.

"Absolutely," I replied.

They chose the last seat because as is generally known the rear end of coaster train can give the biggest thrill. I waited a couple of minutes, hoping to get more riders but knowing that it was unlikely. I released the brake and the train grabbed hold of the lift chain and started its ascent. I didn't know it then but that was to be the final ride of the year for the Comet.

Mr. Nielson came out of the office went into the arcade. Butch joined him as they walked from ride to ride, thanking the operators for their loyalty and dedication. I could see them smiling and shaking hands. Soon the lights from each ride were extinguished and the darkness I felt started to spread. They came up to the ramp to tell me to close. Mr. Nielson looked at me and asked if I might be interested in working through the winter.

"You could work the ballroom in the bar on weekends and after classes at college you could come to help. There's always something that needs doing here," he said.

Without hesitation, I enthusiastically responded, "Yes sir!"

The following day, paychecks would be available for pick up after one in the afternoon. I drove down, parked in my usual spot, and walked through the now silent park to the office. I saw Herb come out of the office holding his check.

"Maybe I'll see you next year," he said, giving my shoulder a squeeze.

He told me he was leaving later that day to get back to his sister's home. As I looked over the midway, I saw that the tent for Mary's Palm Reading was gone. I was sorry that I didn't have the opportunity to say goodbye.

Before going into the office, I took a side trip to the refreshment stand to say my farewells to Red and Helen. They had a house in Florida near St. Petersburg. Red managed the food services at a dog racing track there. Red came out of the stand gave me a hug and told me if I ever made it to St. Pete's to give him a call. I went in the office saw that Helen and Monica were busy with tabulating accounts. I said goodbye, turned, and headed to my car.

Before leaving, I turned and looked at the park. My first season had been an education. I met people who were so different and yet so similar. My Catholic school upbringing and Prep schooling had been put to use. I had the opportunity to learn that the world is a colorful, wonderful place. I would miss Red and Helen, Butch, Elsa, Lou, Nevada, and Ruth as well as Mary and Leo. Justin the tall, kind Russian man reminded me that people of different ethnicities were not the enemies. There were so many other people who affected me that year that all became part of the book of my life. I can't forget Mr. Nielson who never lost faith in me and gave me the opportunity to grow and become the person I am today.

CHAPTER FOURTEEN

A couple of days later, I began my college studies. My schedule included courses in political science, philosophy, English, sociology, history, theology, and education. It was a challenging but appealing first semester. Prep proved to be outstanding preparation for college. My attitude for my studies had improved. I worked harder, was not afraid to participate in discussions, and loved the intellectual atmosphere college presented. My grades reflected my improved attitude.

I worked at the park almost every day. Sometimes I raked leaves while other days I might be needed to run errands. One time I worked on whitewashing the walls of the ballroom. I was happy. On weekends, when the ballroom was hosting an affair, I would work the bar. We would sell set-ups, ice, chips, pretzels, and other snacks. Elsa worked the cloak room while Nevada was the cashier. It was great listening to the big band music that filled the hall. Mike would be a little annoyed at me for working so much.

When I was free, Mike and I would continue our adventures. On Saturdays at the college there would be a mixer in the student lounge that was open to all girls in the community. The Gem City was home to two girls' colleges which meant there would be plenty of opportunity for meeting girls. The lounge was in the basement of a building where the cafeteria was located.

When going down the steps besides the loud music, noisy chatter, and laughter, one entered a cloud of smoke. It seemed that everyone in college smoked which meant my penchant for Marlboros meant I was part of the in crowd.

The semester went by quickly, leading to another and another. I turned twenty-one and Mike and I took our celebration to the tavern we liked so much. Now, we were able to continue our quest to taste every one of the alcoholic concoctions listed in alphabetical order. Manhattans, margaritas, and martinis were next on the list. We celebrated till midnight and Mike drove me home. Reaching twenty-one was a big milestone.

Mr. Nielson called me to his office one day. He told me that he recognized the fact that I did not have a car. He told me I could take the park station wagon and use it as my own with the one condition that I remember painted on the side of both front doors in gold lettering was "Waldameer Park". I used that vehicle for the next two years.

It's strange seeing the midway covered by inches of snow. Real wet snow, not like the "snow" from the cottonwood trees. The Comet track was completely covered. The skeleton of the rides left took on strange, eerie shapes. The vehicle cars and engines were all safely stored away until spring thaw. If you listened hard, you could hear when the wind blew, the sound of laughing children or the screams emanating from the Comet.

College graduation was near. I wanted to go on to law school. Financially, it would have been difficult even with the financial aid that was offered. I did see an interesting alternative. Temple University in Philadelphia was sponsoring a special program that if you worked for two years in the schools of that city it would offer a master's degree in special education. With the money I earned teaching, I could not only get a master's degree but also pave the way for law school. I decided to apply.

It didn't take long to get the notification that I was accepted to the program. I was to report to start classes on August first. That meant I had to leave my job at the park as well as leaving behind my family and friends. I hadn't been a ride operator for a while and before I left, my hope was to run the Comet one last time. I got that opportunity soon after requesting it. I arrived early in the morning, headed straight up the ramp, and jumped over the track to the control levers. I was set to walk the track one more time. It didn't get any easier. I still hated heights. I still hung on the guard rail, fearful of letting go. I still looked at my feet as step by step I made my way back to the station. The difference now though was that even though I was still uneasy in my mind, I knew I could do it.

Goodbyes are never easy. I walked the midway, saying goodbye to all my friends and remembering those that were there that first season. Elsa, Lou, and Justin had passed away. Herb never returned after that year and no one had any information about him. Leo and Mary had also never returned. They had been fixtures at the park for many years. Rumor had it that the Roma people had moved to Atlantic City. Things change. Life goes on.

My parents, brothers, and grandparents drove me to the airport. My life would soon change forever. When the flew over, I could see Waldameer Park down below and I felt a tear run down my eye.

The first year of graduate school was noteworthy in that this was the day I met Diane, my future bride. It didn't start well, however. When I was introducing myself to her as she was seated at a table in the cafeteria. I reached over to shake her hand and knocked her iced tea into her lap. Fifty-three years later, she will still bring that upon occasion.

I finished graduate school and continued teaching special needs children for the next thirty-four years. Looking back over those years, I am grateful to God that I have so many great memories.

Mike and I said our goodbyes the night before. We went out to our place as usual even sitting at our favorite booth. I don't remember where we were in our list of mixed drinks, but I do know we hadn't reached the zs. We talked and laughed. I drove Mike home. He wished me luck and warned me about the dangers of living in a big city like Philly.

"See ya!" He turned and headed to his door.

We left not knowing if or when we would meet again.

Mike was my best man at my wedding. It was so good to be reunited with my best friend on this special day. My wedding was simple and cheap. Diane was not Catholic, and her parents did not look kindly on her marrying one. They weren't comfortable with having a Catholic wedding in their hometown, so Diane and I arranged to have it in Philadelphia. St. James Church was three blocks away from her apartment in an area that was being redeveloped by the

University of Pennsylvania. St. James was a church without a parish. The caretaker pastor was an elderly retired priest. He eagerly agreed to do the service. There was never a word spoken about classes or counselling. He asked if Diane was baptized, and her affirmative answer was enough for him. My parents, Uncle Al, Diane's parents, her grandfather, and her younger brother along with a few friends and Mike, my best man, and Jenny, Diane's best friend, made up our guests.

The night before, Mike and I went to a neighborhood bar. He looked me in the eye and said he had something important to say that he thought I should know.

"I'm gay."

I sat there dumbfounded. How was this possible? Mike was the chick magnet. He charmed every girl we met. Of course, there was also his long and tempestuous relationship with Jill. I didn't know what to say or how to respond.

I laughed and said that we'd better get going. "I've got a big day tomorrow."

Our reception, if you can call it that, was at the house I lived in with my two Jewish roommates, Mickey and Alvin. They were two great guys straight out of Brooklyn. Diane and I had hired a caterer out of south Philly and ordered a typical Italian style service of cheesesteaks, subs, and the typical extras. We bought a case of beer and three or four bottles of wine and one bottle of champagne. We splurged on the champagne, spending fifteen bucks for the bottle. We bought a cake from a nearby bakery. We decorated the living room with white paper bells and crepe paper. It was a real elegant, first-class affair.

It was time to go. I kissed my parents, hugged my dear Uncle Al, kissed my new mother-in-law, and shook hands with my father-in-law. We said our goodbyes. We told my roommates to take good care of our two cats, Caesar and Ralph, and turned to leave. Mike looked me in the face with tears in his eyes and we left for our honeymoon to begin my new life.

I only heard from Mike a couple of times in the years since. I feel ashamed that I didn't make more of an effort. It's easy to blame circumstances. I was too busy. I had to work or I was too tired, plus a million other excuses. Mike was a great friend. He was always kind, generous, and adventurous. He never criticized me or made me feel unhappy.

I'm sorry, Mike.

CHAPTER FIFTEEN

Every classic story has a part called the denouement. It's the part at the end of a story where the author can clarify and complete the missing parts. This is where unanswered questions are finally answered. There are questions that might remain unresolved.

Did I ever answer my mother's inquiry into what Waldameer Park was paying me? To be honest, I don't remember. It was enough to provide me with a little spending money, making me a bit more independent. Probably I don't remember because I would have worked at the park for free if it came to that.

Did I ever learn to play the trombone? Absolutely not! My beloved wife will verify that I have no aptitude for music. Even our dogs fold their ears and leave the room when I try to sing. I do sing the hymns in church, believing that those nearby me in the congregation will just have to tolerate it out of Christian love and compassion. The divine has no choice. After all, He is responsible!

Did I ever learn to swim? Like a rock. I avoid swimming pools. Beaches are for walking and birdwatching, never for swimming.

Can I do jumping jacks? Why would I want to? We worked with a trainer who had me do balance exercises as well as upper body exercises. I still am not coordinated enough to do jumping jacks.

Did I ever find out what calculus was and what was its purpose? Yes, I did. Calculus is the study of the rate of changes related by function. A simple example is:

Faith, Family, Friends, Waldameer Park, plus Diane = Me

Dr. Tower would be proud!

EPILOGUE

I retired in June 2001 after thirty-four years of service working with special needs children. The following are my remarks at my retirement dinner.

My very first real job while I was in high school was at Waldameer Park in my hometown of Erie, Pennsylvania. One of my jobs eventually came to be running the Comet, the park's roller coaster. I remember my great excitement when Mr. Nelson, the park manager, and Butch, the park superintendent, took me to the Comet and told me that I was going to be the operator of what was then the park's signature attraction. In those days, all the braking was done by hand. There were two levers. One to release the train to the hill and the second lever to brake it upon its return. It was thrilling to look up the drive hill and hear the train attach to the chain that would pull it to the top. Then it would disappear in a whir as it made its way around the track with the sound of happy screaming as it completed its journey. I really loved my first day. Operating the Comet was the most prestigious ride at the park and this summer it was all mine!

At the end of the day, Butch told me that as part of my responsibility there was to walk the track each morning checking it for debris or any other hindrance to ensure that would be safe to operate. I am and was then dreadfully afraid of heights. This was like a bombshell. I recall not being able to sleep that night anxiously anticipating this part of the job. *How could I do it?* I wondered. I wanted this job so badly and nervous about the journey I was about to take and the obstacle that stood before it.

The next morning, I got to the park early. The maintenance crew was busy washing the midway, doing maintenance on some rides while others were working on the landscaping and gardens. I walked slowly and uneasily to the Comet. The ride seemed to glare at me and I swear I heard it taunt me by saying, "Mr. Hotshot, The Big Guy's afraid, is he?"

I stared back and said over and over, "I can do this; I can do this."

Slowly, I began to climb the first hill, the lift hill, gripping the guard rail while watching my feet as I put one foot in front of the other. The catwalk seemed narrower than I anticipated and the hill seemed bigger. The first hill is the tallest and to me the most challenging. If I can conquer this the rest should be easy. I dared not look right or left focused on the track making sure it was clear and on my feet. Sweat was pouring off me getting in my eyes as I climbed higher and higher. Up, up, and up till at long last I reached the summit. As I edged to the bend, I was momentarily stunned. The downside would be even more challenging. It was steep and as I peered down it seemed endless. I gathered my courage and slowly and carefully I made my way down saying my Hail Mary's with each step. I don't recall how I did it, but each step led me until the end was in front of me.

Today, I see the station in front of me once more. For thirty-four years I've walked the track always wary and a little afraid of the challenges that stood before me, yet always putting one foot in front of the other, making my way forward. Little did I know that the lessons I learned as a boy some forty years before would serve me so well in my life and career. There have been innumerable challenges to face through my career but somehow, I was able to overcome my weaknesses and fears and go forward. My career here is ending. I've arrived at the station and looking out toward the horizon I see another coaster bigger and higher. Maybe I'll try that one. Thanks to all of you for being my guardrail over the years and putting up with my foibles and failings. It has been a joy and an honor to have worked with my kids and with all of you. And oh yes, just remember to put one foot in front of the other, hold on to the guard rail, and move forward! God Bless!